The Mystique of a Romance Between May & Me

Written by: Tina Gheisari
English version edited by: Michael K. Bender

The Mystique of a Romance
Between May & Me
Author: Tina Gheisari

2016 © Tina Gheisari
All Rights Reserved
All rights reserved. No part of this book may be reproduced or transmitted in any form or by any means, electronic or mechanical, including photocopying and recording, or by any information storage and retrieval system, without permission in writing from the author

---

Editor: Michael K. Bender
Illustrator: Hanieh Barazande
Graphic designer: Behzad Noori

ISBN: 978-1942912101
Publisher: Supreme Art; USA

About the Author

Tina Gheisari, lives in Shiraz, Iran and her native language is Farsi. She has more than 15 years' experience teaching and translating English. Tina is the loving and caring mother of two grown children, a daughter and a son, Hanieh and Hossein, are the source of the inspiration for her novels. Tina believes that children are truly the fruits of their mother's labor and that we all need to remember our mothers in our thoughts and prayers. By sharing her insightful concepts with her readers, Tina keeps the flames in her heart alive. She invites everyone to share their thoughts and inspiration with her

at: TinaGheisari@yahoo.com

Contents

1. Dedication —————————————————————— V
2. Introduction ————————————————————— VII
3. Chapter 1 " Debate: Free Will or Determinism" ———— 1
4. Chapter 2 "Pearl and Shell's Commitment of Love" — 9
5. Chapter 3 "Readiness"——————————————————— 17
6. Chapter 4 "Transformation"————————————————— 25
7. Chapter 5 "Childhood"————————————————————— 33
8. Chapter 6 "A Mystical Conversation" ————————— 43
9. Chapter 7 "Unification" ——————————————————— 51

Dedication

When I was just 17 years old, I made my first journey abroad. Unlike many of my friends in my little town, I could not wait to see and experience the world. So, when I arrived in Japan, besides traveling to see the sights and learning about its history, I had a mission to buy one very special gift, a string of the most beautiful pearls for my mother. Someone guided me to Mikimoto Pearl Island in Japan. There, I watched as divers went into the water retrieving and opening shells, revealing beautiful pearls inside a very unassuming and dark outer protection. At their store, I found the most beautiful string of pink pearls for my mother. For the rest of the journey I could not wait to return home and see my mother's eyes when she would first see the strand of pink pearls. When I finally arrived home some two months later, I had a suitcase full of gifts, but only one mattered.

I will never forget the look in my mother's eyes; it was not the monetary value that was reflected in her eyes but the beauty of the pearls which had accompanied me on my long journey. Their final destination was the physical demonstration of my love for my mother. Pearls, somehow are connected to motherhood. Tina's book tells the heretofore secret of that connection and my connection to her book gave me a renewed spiritual connection to my mother who would have been proud that I had a small role in Tina's outstanding tribute to motherhood and the cycle of life.

    Michael K. Bender
    Haymarket, Virginia
    April 2016

Introduction

True knowledge comes to each of us when we notice how little we understand about life, ourselves, and the world around us. Unknown

More than a half century ago, I began a journey that led me to a place where I would feel comfortable writing an introduction for a magnificent story based on profound Persian wisdom. The pages that follow were written by a teacher in Shiraz, Iran; a person I have never met, but I believe I know very well. Tina Gheisari's book, "The Mystique of a Romance between May and Me," is a beautiful, spiritual and romantic novel. It describes motherhood in a profound and moving way, and includes thoughtful reflection on our choices in life, the meaning of life and death, how music is a universal language, the true meaning of childhood and the mystery of sleep.

"Don't tell me how educated you are, tell me how much you traveled." ~ Prophet Mohammed

When I was a young child, my grandfather would sit me on his knee and turn my attention to a mysterious box, telling me that this little wooden box linked us to people from all over the world. That mysterious wooden box, which he would one day leave for me after his death, was a shortwave radio; a radio which actually received broadcasts from around the world. But, it was not just the wooden box which guided me on a path throughout life; it was his sage advice. My grandfather encouraged me, first through a stamp collection with stamps from around the world, and then through international broadcasts, to pay attention to others, whether or not they believed or thought the same as I did. He said that no one is born with all the answers, but everyone is born with the ability to learn. "Once you learn, you must help others learn, but never will you be always right. So explore the world and look through the eyes of others realizing we all see the same thing, just in different ways, he told me."

Today, we no longer need shortwave radios to explore the world. Travel has become routine and we have the Internet with all the good and bad it brings to us. For me, I have used the Internet to learn and follow my grandfather's advice, which brings me to how I came to know and respect Tina for her work as a writer, teacher and loving mother. Mothers have an advantage over all of us; they are self-educated in teaching skills because they teach on a daily basis.

While exploring my contacts on a business networking site which I now use to connect to the world, (since I no longer travel), I was intrigued by Tina's description of a book she had written in Farsi and I asked her if it was available in English. She sent me a draft, explaining that it had not been edited in English yet, but she told me that I was welcome to read the draft.

I am not the same having seen the moon shine on the other side of the world – Mary Anne Radmacher

So inspired by her story and the lessons I learned from it, I offered to edit her book since, having traveled throughout the world observing other cultures, I thought I might be able to capture the essence of what was obviously so beautifully expressed in her native language.

It is one thing to correct grammar which has lots of rules and exceptions, but editing a truly insightful work from another culture and language requires more than English skills. Only a person with a deep passion and understanding for what the words represent can transform thoughts into a second language. I donated my time to this endeavor because I believed that Tina had somehow managed to give all of us an opportunity to gain an understanding of the beauty of motherhood and mothers, our freedom to choose, the Eastern philosophy of love, and the spiritual being who protects us all. For those of us who are not mothers, Tina's book gives us a greater appreciation for our own mothers and our role in the world in which we live.

Yesterday I was clever, so I wanted to change the world. Today I am wise, so I am changing myself- Unknown

I always had a simplistic approach to God and our relationship with Him. We are all connected, I believe, by a spiritual core. Where we differ from each other, and have differed, is how we are connected to the core of our being. Early in history, philosophers guided people on how to live their lives. As religions developed, the religious leaders provided people with closer spiritual connections and guidelines on how people must live their lives.

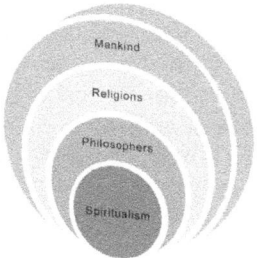

Illustration by Michael K. Bender©

Tina's book, like none other, provides us with a vision of more than a superficial relationship between ourselves and God. She shows us how our daily life has a purpose and how we have a responsibility for others; for that we should grateful to her. As for me:

"I am not the same having seen the moon shine on the other side of the world" – Mary Anne Radmacher

As Socrates told his students, his purpose was not to teach anything but simply to make them think. After reading Tina's book, I have not stopped thinking nor will the readers.

A great and wonderful burden has been lifted from my shoulders because Tina recently wrote to me: "Michael! Wow! Very well done! It couldn't be better! Profound Persian thoughts in a professional and literal American frame!" That is my wonderful reward; I have captured what Tina intended for the readers of this uplifting book. As you read through the pages and finish the book, you will discover that the journey has only begun; there is no ending, just the continuance of the cycle of life.

Michael K. Bender
Haymarket, Virginia
April 2016

"...A great gift has been made to each and every one of us—the privilege of living in the world for a short span of years and the opportunity of doing our part to help the less fortunate; to improve civilization; to advance knowledge, both the scientific knowledge of men and the wisdom which is from above. The gift of human life and the opportunity which is ours to serve others...should be regarded as a sacred trust." George Pepperdine Founder of Pepperdine University

mkbender@outlook.com

Chapter 1
Debate: Free Will or Determinism

"You will never be on your own. We will protect you as a shell which lovingly cuddles its beautiful pearl constantly, and we will accompany you through hurricanes, and violent ocean waves, with compassion for a boat drifting alone on the surface of the lonely sea," a soft voice whispered into Pearl's heart. This heavenly message, which was meant to reassure her, actually frightened Pearl who asked, "Horrible waves?" "Yes" came the response. "You are a pearl, and you were born in the sea, where the realm of adventure lies. But don't panic, because your evolution lies on the crest of waves." "Crest of waves?" Pearl asked. "Yes, you could be as glorious as us," the sound declared.

From the tone of affection and kindness, Pearl discovered that there was a hint of free will; because it said, "…you could be…" As the conversation continued, more questions were raised for little Pearl. "Is there any other choice for me?" Pearl asked. And the pious sound replied, "Yes there is. You might stay inside your pleasant and comfortable shell permanently, and never step out of your shelly world. In that case, you would never achieve the heights that have been determined for you." "And what is that height," Pearl asked. To which the voice replied,"

Becoming a glamorous PEARL in the world, stepping out from being subjective to an objective position. If you come out of your shelter and face the challenges of a crescendo of waves, if you come out of the darkness and allow your brave heart to face the world, you will become the one that you were supposed to be." Pondering deeply on what was said, Pearl answered, "You see, you already call me 'Pearl,' so I am already a pearl. Also, you said that I 'could' be the one that I am supposed to be. So I ask you, "What if I cannot or will not do what you say I should? I don't even know your name. What is your approach: Determinism or free will?" On the one hand, you mention that I have free will to determine what I want to be, but on the other hand, you say that I also have free will to decide what I want to be even though you seem to have determined what I should become."

The question seemed intriguing to the unknown voice. So it inhaled, then exhaled deeply, became philosophical and started its expression while it was clearing its throat. "I was in a meeting one day which was full of different types of people who were there to hear a debate on what governs the world: Determinism or free will? Suddenly, one of the supporters of determinism grabbed the opportunity to talk among the tumult and said, 'Before anything else I would say that the laws of nature and whatever governs the whole universe is reasonable enough to say that a universal system is governing with a determined pattern. We determinists believe that there is a strict and defined organization which determines the way things are and the way things will be. When we say this, however, we mean the whole cosmos and whatever and whoever is involved.'

One of the participants asked, "Can you give us a more detailed example? 'Yes', he replied, 'I can point to the earth and a smaller part of it, for instance, where the laws of physics are absolutely essential. Gravity, for example, affects all objects.' At this moment, one of the members of the audience interrupted, declaring, 'Gravity? Doesn't it exist even beyond the earth, as its attraction has expanded from the smallest atoms to the biggest planets, stars, until all the Universe? Hence, it would be better to say that the force that holds the solar system is the sun's gravitational force!' "Exactly," he signaled his approval by adding, "As you see, no rule should be underestimated, because they are undoubtedly essential and the cosmos is surrounded by them. Therefore, we believe that everything is already determined." Someone then asked, "Does it mean that there are other possibilities for the events in the world when we say that all of them are already determined?' That is correct. You understood it!' he replied. "That is how events could be estimated in the past, assessed in the present, and predicted in the future." One of the more neutral participants commented, "Although this approach is an epistemological issue on the surface, it has a metaphysical nature as one delves deeper." At this point, one member of the audience asked, with a look of frustration on her face, "What is epistemological?" 'It is a Greek term that describes a branch of philosophy that studies the nature of knowledge," he replied, 'If we say that this is a metaphysical matter, it means that in determinism, stable laws which determine whatever we don't know, or even we cannot know, govern and organize the future of the whole universe. So we will be able to predict the future of the universe if we achieve the required information about the laws of nature governing it.'"

Now, a profound thoughtful silence filled the atmosphere as the audience realized that the voice was saying that everyone should know that a chance to speak should be given to non-determinists.

One of the participants whose face had become rosy and was thinking that there was no necessity for an introduction, started his speech confidently, "We're free to decide according to our own free will. Who can deny this gift which has been given to human beings? Although we are affected by different factors such as the circumstances of our upbringing, geography, etc., we are the ones who eventually choose." One member of the audience asked boldly, "Does it mean that we are free once we make a decision?"

"I suggest that you hold on a bit so that you may challenge the situation, and then make no decision. You will quickly learn that there hasn't been any other choice than the one that you were already about to receive. It is better to give an example to make it clearer. Imagine a shiny day that you have awakened very energetic. You have three important items on your agenda, but with your limited time you can only do one of them. You do not know how to prioritize them. These three items are:

1. To repair your child's dress
2. To go to a party
3. To discuss a work matter with one of your colleagues

You look at the to-do-list and would probably think, 'Well I can choose any one I want because I am given free will.' But if you let go and follow a natural flow, and you don't have any preconception toward any of the activities (which definitely takes a little courage) then you would see that:

1. The needle is broken, so you are not able to repair your child's dress.
2. ...
3. The phone of a colleague who you were trying to call to have a discussion with, is switched off.

In the end, the second option (which was participating in a party) would be the only option that remains."

"Perhaps the second option seemed to have the least

importance at first. But as you have noticed it became the only one. Well, how can you prove that you had free will? Or even if you had chosen one of three options at first, how do you know which one was the best? What if I chose to do none of them?"

The non-determinist voiced opposition at this moment and said, "This is not fair. It is obviously understandable that you made up your examples in a way in which you can have your desired outcome, to already show that two other options (option number one and three) were not really options, but just matters to be ignored; to say that option number two was the only possibility which is called an obligation. Anyone would simply know that I could select any of them! Now, I can say that I have an incurable chronic illness, for instance, and eating sweets is as bad as poison for me. And I know it. Yet I eat a bar of chocolate as I have free will to do as I wish."

At this moment, the people were surprised by a shy woman in a pretty, simple dress and ponytail who started to talk modestly, "I am a mother, and not so well educated as you. But I want to give you an example of my motherhood so that this debate gets a little bit easier: I designed my house according to my children's needs, interests, desires, as well as their strengths and weaknesses; this means that, while they are still young, there are not any fragile objects available to them; no breakable glasses or plates, no chemicals, etc. Also, I provide whatever they need. For example, their foods, their drinks, their medicine all at the right time. I do let them be free to go to any part of the house, to touch whatever they like, and to eat and drink whatever they want in such a safe environment which is designed especially for them as I believe in my ability to design a house safe for my children. I am confident that I have provided for them in a way that they will be protected from any harm. As a mother, I may say that I have given the gift of freedom to my children inside a lovely platform which is based on my motherhood."

Little Pearl, who was listening to the tedious explanation from the unknown voice for quite a while, and was becoming impatient, found the smart mother's point of view very pleasing. So, Pearl interrupted the unknown voice and said, "I think I have free will which is surrounded by the limitation of your love." The unknown voice indicated its approval and ended the discussion. Perhaps, it had understood that such hard moments had been frustrating for new Pearl. Consequently, it calmly left the Pearl alone. Pearl was still thinking of the voice's discussion while it's beautiful eyes had become really sleepy. Then it moaned, "Oh my goodness, who is responsible for this insomnia that I have now? The one whose sound fills my heart full of warm thoughts, and its wisdom is stealing my sweet sleep? But I don't care, as I am fascinated with a new understanding of free will and determinism, even if the price is sleeplessness."

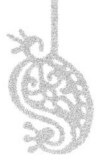

Chapter 2
Pearl and Shell's Commitment of Love

"The two most important days in your life are the day you are born and the day you find out why."

Mark Twain

Glamorous Pearl had intended to sleep since there was no longer any noise coming from anywhere. The continuous flow of messages of wisdom finally paused. Now, there was just Pearl, who found itself alone and in silence. It seemed that all the conditions were ripe for a sound sleep. So, it closed its eyes hoping to have a good night, but it was not to be. Pearl felt an intense, inner sound beating inside its inner world, now stronger than ever. Sad, exhausted Pearl pressed its eyelids firmly as if its eyes could reduce the volume of the sound; yet, the more it pressed its eyelids, the more understandable and clearer the sound became. It was a strange feeling; Pearl was sleepy when it opened its eyes, and perfectly awake when it closed them. Its body was tired but it now was determined to stay up, full of motivation like a knight preparing for battle while its mind was telling it to crawl back into bed and sleep. It was already exhausted at the thought of a breathtaking battle which might lay ahead. But why a battle? Was not Pearl regarded as a creation which was given the gift of free will? If so, then it should be free to accept or reject this responsibility! Or, as it believed, was this free will restricted by determinism?

Because we cannot measure the things that have the

most meaning, we give the most meaning to the things we can measure. Fred Hargadon

Pearl liked to ignore all these conflicts assuming it was free to make choices. But, could it simply forget about its passion for being carried along the surf to pursue so many attractive unfolding, mysterious adventures? So, it thought, "I could win, or I could lose! Who knows? But are these words just comparative terms which simply suggest my silly illusions? Are not comparative concepts about materials and their functions just measurement without any redeeming values? While I am a Pearl, my originality is the sea, and the sea is a realm of endlessness. I am told that I can become as wonderful as them although I am not sure I know fully what being them will mean. If what they have said is true, then I would be endless; the same as them. How do the comparative terms which refer to measurement apply to me? Well, if I pull the trigger, and am not concerned about winning or losing, then I will be out of any shackles, and get rid of fears about winning or losing."

Suddenly, an inner voice began deep inside Pearl, and it was pointing out Pearl's lack of ability, "Have you ever looked at your skinny body? It is very small and vulnerable! Look at your shell which has been always surrounding you carefully! Do you know that you will be lost if it doesn't support you even for just for a second? You might be destroyed by sea invaders. Have you gotten so much self-confidence that you will step in the way of starting this challenge? Or is it wisdom which orders you to stay in your secure shelter and not take these risks? Compare your little body with the huge waves. Then you will come to the conclusion that "pulling this trigger" might not be lucky."

"You are hearing just a whisper. Do you really want to follow just a whisper? While you don't know if you can trust the source of these word, you also cannot know how much it is committed to its words. How do you know if the voice is honest? Are you confident that it won't leave you midway in the journey? What happens if it does?! You have already lost your kind shell, ruined your honorable past, and ultimately would be lost in the vast ocean without anything to protect you!"

Being discriminating is easy with a crystal clear heart. Although it was just a little pearl, its essence was from the sea, so it was definitely smart in discriminating different sounds and their sources. It believed intuitively that this inner voice had a lower tone in comparison to the spiritual caller, but it had no reason or explanation for its origin.

It understood correctly that what was making it waiver once more was comparison; comparing its little body with a huge ocean. "Oh God, assessment and measurement again," Pearl mourned. So it screamed, "Hey! Although I am so little and still young, I understand that winning, losing, comparing, assessing, measuring big and small are all physical terms. And I know that my body is physically well. Materialism will be my destiny if I stay in my shell and choose to be static."

"However if I can step out of my shelter, team up with ocean waves, and trust my protective guidance, I will go beyond all these limited terms and be unified as one with the ocean; this victory has already been promised to me."

At this moment, another conversation began and it startled Pearl. It was Shell, the constant supporter and protector who was always pampering Pearl with lots of kindness and love and and providing a constant defensive shield around her. It started moaning softly, "This is Shell, who is talking to you; Shell, your warm home. I express my grief to you boldly and frankly. How can I hide my feelings? I used to take care of you all night long and take care of your needs all day long. I harmonized my being with yours with all of my love and cuddled you gently to protect you from the strangers and invaders. How could you leave me having been cared for in this way by me? How could you travel? What didn't I do for you? Which emotion did I deprive you of? Why are you so full of this temptation; a temptation of motion? Have you ever been concerned about what happens to me after you leave? Can you imagine my situation without you? Oh, baby! Shell without Pearl means the beginning of emptiness for me"

This emotional challenge was not one which could be neglected. Shell was right! And everything it said was the truth. Shell was the basic home where Pearl had been born and grew up. Pearl had been taught to feel, to think, to understand, and to imagine, all by Shell; such a compassionate mother and teacher! What should it do now, faced with this much love and pain?

Love was a precious heritage which was transferred from the Shell's soul to Pearl's. So Pearl had no way but to calm the anguished heart of Shell.

"Oh my beautiful Shell, you are so unique in your purity. I always adore you and I am so proud of you. Stay calm for the sake of goodness! I did not see this much flame in your heart. I know that this path and this separation would not be easy. Most of us like their past and identify closely with it. I also know that life will become full of breathtaking events once I am out from under your protective, umbrella cover. But I am confident that you will get higher in this path as well as me, as we are going to follow a heavenly director along the way. I have a feeling that you will become more spiritual than me. I have no doubt."

It seemed as if enormous patience and acceptance was all that Shell needed in confronting this vital decision. However, it took time for Shell to give up resisting and calm down. Finally, it became silent as it was aware that Pearl - its flesh and blood - had a strong challenge which lay ahead. Pearl needed a deep and sound sleep. So this peaceful quiet made the poor little, panicked Pearl sleep.

Sleep is a mysterious time; it is a time when we let go and let our being be surrounded by a higher power; it is much the same as a client who trusts an experienced healer, because he believes in healing. Sleep is when ego withdraws and blocks both resistance and interference. Healing becomes much more productive and effective. Sleep is when spiritual healers find an opportunity to release wounds from our body.

Pearl and Shell opened their eyes in the morning and they were both feeling better than last night. It was as though some of their distress had been washed away by means of pure water; a magic flow which is called healing.

Shell started the conversation this time, with more visible patience and strength. "Hey, my sweetheart! Let's make a promise, not sadly, but firmly." "Which promise from my heart, oh my mother?" Pearl asked obediently. "My mother?" Shell questioned, "What is this passionate word that goes to my core?" Pearl continued, "One day, I was in the realm of the Supreme Power. He spoke to me graciously, "Listen my little dear, I want to give you a precious gift with which you can communicate with others not just me, so you may express the flashes of love that you have hidden in your heart. You could change the world through this wonderful tool." So I asked, "And what is this gift?" "This gift is language!' was the reply: 'A tool by which you may convert passives to actives, and abstracts to concretes. In fact, this tool is a form of magic. But if it is used too much, its magic will be diminished, like so many other gifts. Hence, give me two promises right away: First, keep in your mind that language is a gift that is given to you by me and for this reason it must be acknowledged. Second, use language just for making things better; never destroy anyone or anything else by means of language; never use it for insulting or breaking a heart, as it is given to you and can be taken back; you lose it if you misuse it." I said, "Ok!" Then, he said, 'Well done my Pearl. Now you may know that language consists of words."

He started teaching me the words gradually, 'The first word you must learn is 'love' because this is the essence of me; the glittering flames from which the Creation has been started; the flash that I put inside the heart of all of my creatures to keep the Universe permanently alive. After that I created a generous protector from the same species to ensure their survival. I called this caring supporter, 'Mother.' "That is why this is such an amazing word." Pearl said. They both became silent for a moment. In fact, Pearl and Shell were talking using abstract language now. They were talking through the sounds of their hearts. Finally, Pearl broke the icy silence and said, "We were about to make a promise!" Then Shell, the Mother, spoke up and said, "Ah yes! You should promise not to forget this enamored love wherever you go, and whatever you become." "I promise mother, I do." Pearl answered!

Chapter 3
Readiness

Pearl's heart was on the fire with a burning and demanding desire. The caller was drawn to this desire like a magnet. "Hello, Pearl." The caller said. And Pearl answered, "Hello, stranger." "Am I a stranger?" the caller asked woefully. "Am I a stranger despite the fact that I connect to you every second? Am I a stranger when I rush to you once I feel the flames of your heart from so far away? Who can hear you while you are silent? Who can read the secret in your heart when you haven't written it yet? Although I am absent from time to time, I am still like a splendid sun which has surrounded your world warmly, making you alive with its golden lights even if clouds seem to put some barriers between us. Never depend upon knowing my name, seeing or staring at me in this relationship, as it is beyond these insignificant things." The warmth and honesty of the caller's words stimulated the innocent heart of the Pearl.

Pearl's face became like a velvet rose. Then the caller continued, "What is your plan? What is on your mind? Will you select staying or traveling?" Pearl started talking while her face was blushing, "How can I select staying when I see you pursuing this journey so strongly? The temptation of this path has already made me agitated and unsettled; I cannot sleep with all the excitement. I count the moments impatiently, and I seek you passionately until you hold my hands and ride me over and through the waves. The passion of this dangerous journey has faded and overwhelmed the confidence of staying. I prefer the path to another life which is risky, instead of the safe one I have now. This desire has stolen my night's sleep. Anyway, I intend to put all my trust in you and want to come with you. Although I will have a challenging and difficult path, I will cope with the different challenges, and I am aware that the destination is very far away. Yet, I still desire to travel with you. In fact, I don't wonder about the destination; I wonder about the exciting adventures along the way. I am not worried about taking a shortcut, as the longer journey with a friend and protector, the better."

The more Pearl talked, the more the caller became confident that choosing Pearl was a perfect selection. It was getting more and more obvious that the destination would be prosperous indeed, and they would get to the land of light, at last. The caller, with a contented voice asked Pearl, "Does it mean that you are ready?" and Pearl answered, "Definitely yes! Both my body and my heart are ready!" So the caller glistened with a sense of pride.

The most remarkable part for the caller was that Pearl did not ask when, where, or even how they would travel. Although this point demonstrated the sincerity of Pearl's intention, it put a heavier responsibility on the caller's shoulder but it also caused it to trust Pearl more than ever. It seemed that this was the time to describe the plan for the journey, although the moment was difficult, even for the caller itself. Nonetheless, it was a task that had to be done! After procrastinating, the caller breathed deeply and started the story. "You are a precious pearl which has been chosen by the Almighty, angels, and the Kingdom of

Heaven. And you know how special you are to them. Any traveler needs a rider, and you have been considered the most valuable one. You will be in an amazing situation."

Pearl did not understand anything at all, and fortunately the caller understood this, as its heart was connected to Pearl's. Then it continued its description while Pearl remained silent even though the message was full of ambiguity. "Well, a human being who is settled on the earth is the best form to be a rider because human beings have two aspects: one is physical, and one is spiritual. One is based on materials, and one is based on soul. For this reason, they have both worldly and heavenly components. Sometimes people become involved in their daily routines, and sometimes they remember who they are when they gaze at the sky. So This body will be your form so that you accomplish, through this physical body, whatever is planned in the Cosmic Creation System, where your destiny will be defined and written according to the Divine Order. It means that this material body provides a vehicle through which you may reach your divine life purpose. But keep in mind, always and everywhere honor your body the most, because this is your own tool which gives you the golden opportunity to remove yourself from subjectivity and step into objectivity. Moreover, your body will be like a temple, as it can act like a medium; a bridge between heavenly and earthly creatures; I want to say that you may sometimes find those mourning with broken hearts, and you will deliver their whisper and prayers to the sky, and then receive their responses from heaven and provide them back to the mourners as a healing. Additionally, you may receive a warning from the Lord to awaken the neglected people on the planet so that you make them alive once more. You may even become a link between an ill body and healing angels to treat the people in need. But notice that none of this would be practical unless you purify the temple of your own body!"

Pearl was just listening to the fascinating words of the caller without moving or asking a question; not saying a word. Perhaps, this attentive listening made the caller extremely enthusiastic in its description of what was about to unfold.

It continued, "There is an ashram in which you are supposed to settle; a sensitive window through which the whole universe can be seen and understood." "A sensitive window?" Pearl asked. "What is its name? Why am I supposed to be there?" The caller replied, "Yes, a sensitive window, whose name is Eye. It is astonishingly big, dark, and beautiful. It would be interesting for you to know that you have many similarities with Eye; it means that you correspond with each other; that is why you have been determined to be set there. Human beings' eyes are the perfect perspective through which the cosmos can be viewed, can be known, and can be felt. This knowing and feeling can be the starting point of their spiritual growth and ultimately their connection with the Universe. So be aware that you are really regarded as a reputable, purified, and plain Pearl by the Kingdom of Heaven. Remember Pearl, that eyes get more beautiful when they shed tears." "Tears?" Pearl asked. "Yes" Caller answered, "When people have broken hearts, when they feel a sense of grief, and when they fall in love, they weep. The drops that they shed from their eyes are tears. There have been some correlations between you, eyes, and weeping in the Cosmic System of Creation. That is their reason to place you there Pearl." Pearl asked with a trembling voice, "Do you think that I can be a competent eye? Can I become the one that I am supposed to be?" "Yes, indeed," the caller answered assuredly, "Your essence is from our realm, and you are presumed to be capable to go on this heavenly mission. If you keep purifying your eyes during your lifetime, and keep your sight spiritual forever, then you will grow up as high as the heavens with clairvoyance."

Obscure fears were making Pearl frightened very deep inside, as Pearl was a little passenger that was getting ready for a huge journey. At this moment, Pearl looked at the caller and hesitantly questioned, "I want to talk to you honestly although it seems a little bit late. Thinking of being apart from sea, Shell, and you, makes me panic. Sea, Shell, and you are all I have, and I want to let you know that you are my most beloved possessions. I know my destiny will lead to prosperity as it is written according to the Divine Order. Yet, I cannot simply leave behind my best." So, the caller replied, "Look my sweet Pearl! The necessity of this heavenly path requires patience. Sea, Shell, and I cannot stand being apart from you as well. But, hopefully you will still visit the sea." Pearl then asked, "How about Shell and you?" "There is some news that somehow Shell will be sent to you, but I haven't heard about their policy yet. And this decision is made by them because Shell has been moaning and complaining to God for the bitter days when you will separate from it," the caller answered. "How about you?" Pearl asked "My mission description has been kept secret so far; I know as much about it as you do," the caller answered.

Impulses of love were transformed into embraces. The caller continued, "However my celestial mission is to accompany you until the end, but I don't know for how long or how much time it will take! I just know that at this moment that the most important matter is for you to keep in your heart all subtle issues that I have mentioned to you, and to apply them at the required times. Also, note that temples, coasts, seas, and lakes are defined as our rendezvous to meet and talk. Moreover, we will have urgent meetings if our hearts are broken, or we will have fallen in love; this is for sure."

It was crystal clear that the next words from the caller were its concluding words, "I heard with my own ears that compassionate angels were warning you several times, "Nether Caste ye your pearles before swyne." Pearl asked the caller oddly, "What did you say?" and one more time it repeated it in other words, "Don't Cast Your Pearls before Swine!"

Chapter 4

Transformation

"Faeries, come take me out of this dull world,
For I would ride with you upon the wind,
Run on the top of disheveled tide,
And dance upon the mountains like a flame"

W.B. Yeats

Finally, the splendid sun of the promised day appeared; the glorious day that would have made anyone or anything else impatient. Chosen Pearl was about to be transported from sea to land. The directors of this journey were cosmic creations, the passenger was from the sea, and the host land was earth. So all the residents of heaven, sea, and the earth had become enthusiastically involved in this adventure.

The caller came to the little passenger and asked it gently, "Are you ready?" Pearl answered, "Yes I am." The great moment of transformation is really mysterious. Passengers are the ones who leave everything behind in their motherland, and gaze at the sparkles of hope in a new land. They die in one world and are born in another. But this does not happen unless they close their eyes during their beloved departure, and open them as they are on to a new and exciting destination. It did not matter if the story was about free will or determinism, love or infatuation. Pearl had already pulled the trigger, and had given its heart to the caller, boldly and bravely awaiting it to lead it towards its destiny.

The caller asked Pearl, "Do you know what wings

are?" Pearl answered with a naughty reply, "You tell me what they are." Ignoring Pearl's tone, the caller continued, "Any transformation needs a force, and any transportation demands a dynamic power through which the movement becomes accomplishable; I am supposed to be your wings through this journey according to the Divine Order; the Order which has been from the realm of the Supreme Power. I will pass you over sea, and I will accompany you until you settle down in the final place which will be considered as your virtual end." So, Pearl asked with obvious concern, "... until I settle down in the final place which is considered as my virtual end?" And the wings answered, "Correct! This means that I will give you the power of flight beginning now, and I will fly you to the new land, and I will stay by your side for as long as you ascend in your earthly body." Now, Pearl became sad, and asked, "What about when I settle down? Will you leave me by myself?" Now, the wings had become sad, sharing Pearl's deep concern. It replied, "Oh dear Pearl, as I told you before I only know about the how's and how longs of this path and only as much as you." So, Pearl kept quiet even if the answer was not enough to satisfy its concern.

Suddenly, Pearl felt its body inside a body which was as light as a feather; Pearl was feeling a delightful lightness. Pearl had turned to the heart of a powerful existence that had capability to fly from sea to land. The caller, who was just a medium through which the orders, the warnings, the quotes, and whispers of heavens were sent to Pearl, now had a marvelous pearl in the center of its body, inside its heart; a pearl which had thousands of flames hidden in its heart, thousands of tears unshed, and thousands of words unspoken in the center of the wings.

The splendor of this togetherness, the location of Pearl in the center of wings, led to the start of the journey. Yes, the journey finally began. Flying Pearl or Pearly Bird had now stepped onto a path; a path which did not divulge its end. Now, all the angels and fairies were respectfully gathered around the little passenger, adoring and admiring its decision. They were going to stay by its side throughout the indigo colored seas, to ride with it over big waves, and to help it to somehow touch the blue sky. Meanwhile, Pearl and Wings were talking, laughing, and cheering nonstop through their journey, although their conversation was not perceptible to the large crowd of angels and fairies who were gathered around them, and were applauding loudly. The sounds of dance from the fascinating ocean waves was buffering their talk. Fish, dolphins, corals, seagulls, and all the other sea creatures were greeting them smilingly and offering their congratulations on this wonderful transformation. Flying Pearl or Pearly Bird also was replying to them with a gentle and kind smile. These greetings and salutations provided entertainment along the way, and washed away any distress from the little heart of the traveler, and made the time pass faster than usual.

They had taken off high into the blue sky and it was clearly visible for the flying Pearl. As a matter of fact, the world of Pearl had been expanded; Pearl, the little baby who had emotionally detached from Shell on its own, had passed through sophisticated debates of free will and determinism courageously, and had confidently put all its trust in the heavenly caller. For this courageous decision, it deserved this amazing flight into the sky and the glorious perspective it presented from far above was definitely a well-deserved reward.

While angels, fairies, beautiful dancing waves, and all the sea creatures were still applauding and cheering loudly, Wings screamed, "Hey my Pearl!" then Pearl took a deep breath; it inhaled deeply, and then shouted with all its power and responded, "Yes, baby!" Wings responded, "Look at this blue sky, how shiny, smooth, and endless it is; how free of clouds it is." Pearl replied, "Yes, I see!" Then Wings shouted again, "Keep this image precisely in your heart, because you will have to remember it in the future." "What do you mean?" asked Pearl. "That's all I can say right now, and not more," said Wings, "Just keep in your mind the view of a blue sky which has no clouds." But, as usual, Pearl did not know what Wings was talking about. It just trusted it as always, and stopped asking, and then tried to save the charming image of the blue sky, and shortly got back to the enchanted adventures of sailing in the sky.

A pretty land was starting to become visible. The more the land was appearing, the louder the cheers, salutes, and songs of the crowd of angels and fairies were getting. These songs and rhymes were declarations of a magnificent moment to the whole world; it was like a sweet anxiety that was shaking the tiny heart of our Pearl, and making it beat faster and harder!

Finally, the shining angelic group descended with the chosen Pearl onto the planet. At last, Pearl settled down on the ground. And the outburst of its manifestation was an astonishing moment that no one could deny. One of the angels came closer to sing a song, while the other angels were swirling and whirling around baby Pearl, "We called on you to step out of the realm of nowhere to the realm of being. And your willingness made you respond to our proclamation. So, we as the inhabitants of heavens, seas, and earth, are all gathered together to celebrate this fabulous display. I would like to announce that we are all here to give you a harmonious and beautiful body which captures everyone else's attention and fascinates everyone else's heart; such a lovely soul must have such a unique body. And later, when we meld this special body and soul together into this beautiful shape, and create such an adorable creature, it is our responsibility to cut the hand of devil from you, and protect you against any darkness, maliciousness, or impurities; it means that you will be untouchable by any Satan forever. In the name of the Lord, you will be supported by our graces, and will be embraced with our redemption, and will be surrounded by our light and love. You will be given whatever you desire; so the earth and the whole planet will be at your service, because you have always done whatever we have wanted as well."

As the Great Angel was declaring these words, the other angels were showing their approval of this impressive declaration by nodding their heads, clapping their hands, and whispering heavenly songs. But Pearl seemed an innocent part of the angelic crowd, having no understanding of what was happening. At this moment, the kind caller learned that Pearl had become confused, although Pearl did not express her confusion; not even one word! Consequently, the caller felt that it was time to explain the circumstances to Pearl. It said, "Dear Pearl, this wonderful celebration is held for your sake. You were taken here ceremoniously on angels' hands so that you could settle down in an adorable body which would be harmonious with your beautiful soul. And all of this is because your essence is one of love. And if you are ready to hear the truth, I would like to say that you are the abstract of the whole cosmos." Then caller pointed out a direction, and made Pearl look at something strange.

Oh Lord, a little girl wrapped in a bright sheet; a perspiring, rosy baby whose beautiful big eyes were closed. Now, caller said to Pearl, "Look at this carefully, and then answer my question." Pearl took a deep breath, and said, "Ok!" Then, the caller asked, "Do you like the body? Do you like this body?" Pearl asked, "Should I?" It replied, "Definitely, yes. Because, as we already discussed this will be the temple of your soul, where you will connect the earth to the sky. This will be a tool through which the mission of your divine life will become achievable. So how can you not like it? You must absolutely like it!" After this persuasive statement, Pearl looked at the sleeping baby one more time, but this time with more curiosity and care, it found a real inanimate body before it. Then Pearl questioned, "Why is this baby so pale and motionless? Although it's the ultimate of beauty and tenderness, I can easily feel the sense of a lifeless being." "Very well done my genius Pearl!" the caller said to Pearl. "You are so intelligent Pearl. She had acute pneumonia last week, and she finally passed away today after much pain and suffering. But this is not all; that's just its earthly story. The interesting part of its heavenly story is that the contract of the previous soul was finished after just a short period of time, and it was finished today. Consequently, it is back to the realm of spirits according to the Divine Order. Now, all of this rejoicing is for the sake of your presence here as the one who is responsible for the rest of the path; you are the one who has already accepted a very special mission. Now, let me know if you like this special body!" "I like it very much," Pearl replied. It was an unforgettable moment when the angels applauded loudly right after this positive answer and then they had Pearl walk in the body of the little motionless girl.

"What about you? Will you walk in with me or is it just me? What will be happening with you?" Pearl asked in a sad voice. Caller answered, "This body is your own realm; your private territory. You are the only one who has been permitted to walk in it." She said, "But it's a long time that we have been together. We even became one along the way from sea to land, how about this togetherness, spending time together, sharing feelings?" But the noises from the crowd muffled her voice.

While Caller was disappearing among the crowd, it screamed loudly, "My sweet Pearl, do you remember that

I wanted you to save the image of blue sky in your heart? Someday I will find you, and meet you, and I will have an image of bright blue sky in me, and you will remember me in this way." The unknown voice, the caller, the indicator, the wings, faded out at this moment; this was the bitter moment of a long farewell! Pearl was surrounded by a deadly grief, so she whispered softly, "Hey my kind mate, I am going to miss you very much." Then her heart became broken, and her charming eyes became teary. So she wept. And this was when she was born.

Chapter 5
Childhood

"It's the children the world almost breaks who grow up to save it."

Frank Warren

It was clear to many that the generosity of the Lord could not be complete or even functional in the absence of a mother. But, no one was aware how Shell had been brought into motherhood preceding Pearl's birth. As long as love is in charge, asking about the how's and why's did not seem to matter. However, the innate love and compassion in Shell promoted her from being subjective to an objective state; Shell attained the height of being the finest mother on the planet. As a matter of fact, a mother is the only one who could receive and take care of a little alien creature that had just separated from the angels, and became a human being. Perhaps, on the earth it can be said that a mother is an angelic human who has risen to support and protect a baby.

Forgetting is a sort of tactic utilized by Divine planning so that we become centered and focused on the planet; this means that we rarely remember where we came from, which stage of creation we were in, what were our goals and aims on the planet, and what commitments and promises we made. After all, this forgetfulness or ignorance is a gift that settles us down on the ground with stability, makes us eager to live our life willingly, and puts us on the path of the so-called Divine Program which is designated for each and every of us. Shell was not able to remember anything from the past. Yet, staring at the operating room when a man in a green dress came out hurriedly and happily, and informed her mother about her cute baby girl, "Your little daughter definitely died, my colleagues and I all saw this. But, suddenly there was the presence of something magical in the air and it changed everything, unbelievably. When May opened her eyes, it was absolutely stunning. We are all still shocked."

Her name was "May," a soft little girl who could easily remind others of the fascinating blooming season: May, when the spring breeze tenderly flatters the lovely face of blossoms on the trees; May, when the cave woman, the Mother of nature comes out of the cave of winter and shows off all her beauty to the earth and the skies.

May's eyes were beautiful, big and dark, reflecting a mysterious deep loneliness. She was in her bed and her body was numb, as if she was still feeling the heaviness of her soul changing; vital signs were all indicating that May was alive, her pulse was fine, and it made all the physicians cheerful. Yet, she was too feeble to move, or at least to open her lovely eyes. Her mother was just looking at her beloved daughter in silence while her heart was full of gratitude.

Easy or difficult; time passes. The difficult days of May's sickness passed as well. Now she was growing up in her mother's warm cuddle. May was a pretty little girl with a cute face and slim body. She was gentle, smart, and polite, and these adorable qualities had clearly distinguished her from others; she was like a shiny pearl when she was among her same age group. She used to play with them and do whatever they do, but there were some unknown barriers between the other children and May! And this was an unpleasant, annoying feeling that hurt her because her childish nature had a tendency to cause her to live in a childish way, to jump up and down, to scream, to love ice cream, to be naughty, while her magnificent soul was carrying a heavy feeling on her shoulder which was not in harmony with her childhood silliness. Or, maybe her fragile body was warning her to keep out of these sorts of activities. May's body was completely healthy, but she was mostly tired, exhausted, and bored. While she was playing with her friends, she used to get pale, and this made her mother worry about her. This finally, led her to see doctors who checked her health; several times they said that she was totally healthy after different types of medical tests.

These factors, although they seemed unimportant, caused her to withdraw from others and she became an aloof child, spending the majority of her time in silence. She looked as though there was someone or something waiting for her in her loneliness. When she was among the children, she felt lonely. As a result, she used to leave the crowded places, to a place where she was feeling a warm, lovely and mighty presence by her side. May usually shed tears in bed before she fell asleep. Though she was just a little girl, she was feeling as if she was missing an unknown beloved being; she almost always had this feeling inside. Perhaps, she was able to hear the voice of her caller (in the wonderful moments of transferring from a conscious to an unconscious state right before she fell asleep) that used to say, "Pearl, keep in your mind that eyes get very beautiful when they shed tears." Just remembering a moment of those fascinating conversations would put flames in her heart. She would call her mother to ask her for a glass of cold water late in the night. As she was still so young and was thinking about missing someone, her mind would be healed or relieved with a glass of water.

Water! Water, was always the reminder of love and

freedom for May. She would lose control when she was on the beach. Beach was the only place where May was able to get rid of the heavy loneliness and wash away the feelings of alienation. That is why she constantly kept asking Shell to take her to the beach so that she could swim and play in the sand at the beach. When May was there, she would hear some mysterious sounds even while she was fervently playing on the sand on the beach. It was those moments she would inform her mother about her inner conversations. In the past, Shell used to get worried about her sweet daughter when she had these audio illusions, or any other type of psychic problems. But May did not care about that, and still excited, aroused, and thrilled to be on the beach, because she was familiar with the voices, sounds, and rhythms at the beach more than any other place! As a matter of fact, beach, offshore, and sea were nostalgic places for May although she was not aware of the reasons consciously. This nostalgia was able to fill her heart with joy and happiness but she would not know the reason. May was able to hear the symphony of life from the sea waves. She would feel a genuine connection between her soul to an originality deep inside of her. She used to gaze at the sea in the last moments right before Shell asked her to get ready to go home. Perhaps she was watering the bowl of her thirsty eyes with sparkling drops of sea so she would survive until the next time she could return to sea again.

It would be perfect if all creations were created in harmony with the world. It sometimes seems that a great spiritual mission falls on thin and small shoulders. The delicate body of May was a small cart carrying a large soul on the ground. In spite of the fact that May was still a child, her soul was sensible, conscious, and cognizant. Her nature was drawing her among the other children to play and have fun. On the other hand, the funny and noisy games were tedious and tiresome when viewed from the window of her mature soul. May had a deep and profound understanding of something that deprived her taste of the sweetness of childish days. In other words, she did not and could not live childhood as a normal child!

Although she tried to play the same as any child, she had a keen awareness, even during her times of pleasure. Whenever she opened her mouth to talk about her feelings and what she perceived, the people stared at her abnormally, and it always led her to modify her thinking to theirs or, it sometimes made her give up talking altogether. Poor May! She had so much to say, but she generally had to choose to be silent. May was not shy or aloof in her nature, but it was her circumstances that made her so.

One day, Shell was supposed to go to May's school for a consultation. Shell went there, and listened to the school consultant and she became a little bit panicked. "May seems to have no willingness for learning or education. This caused us to arrange a test to assess her intelligence. Fortunately, the result of the intelligence test shows that there is nothing wrong with her. Yet, we have two problems with May: First, she cannot sufficiently cope with the reality of real life. She is an introverted student, and this separates her from the other classmates, which is not good for her. This inability to properly communicate has caused her to become weak in respect to interaction. As a result, she has lost so many good chances to learn subjects like science, mathematics, geography, etc. So, we urge you to teach her how to understand and touch the physical world. The second issue is that her drawings, paintings, compositions, and other activities show us that she perceives some images and sounds which are extraordinary. As you can see, the latter issue, extraordinary imagination and perception, empowers the former issue, lack of proper communication and interaction with the real and physical world."

Shell was feeling that this was the end. She was discouraged because her sweet beloved child seemed to have gotten herself into trouble. Shell was feeling like giving up as she had seen her cute girl near death with her own eyes some years ago, and she had mourned and prayed to God so much to take her back to life. The consultant's opinion was not something easy to hear. However, she asked sadly, "What is your suggestion? How can I attach her to real life?" The consultant replied, "You must take her to a tougher environment." "What do you mean by a tougher environment?" asked Shell. And the consultant continued, "According to a Chinese approach, everything is either Yin or Yang in the entire universe. All objects, planets, animals, foods, behaviors, people, and even the towns, cities, and countries have two aspects: Yin or Yang. Whatever is cool, cold, calm, dark, fiction, is Yin. Conversely whatever is warm, hot, aggressive, bright, real, is Yang. We are living in a coastal town here. By the way, how does May interact with the sea?" "She loves the sea!" said Shell. "I could already guess." the consultant added, "So I suggest you to take her far from the sea, to somewhere Yang, near to mountains for example. We are hoping that May will become more familiar with reality, so that she becomes more effective in her social communications, and more powerful in her studying, if you do as we suggest."

Shell, like any other mother, was only concerned about her sweetheart. As a result, she decided to move to another place without hesitation. But she had to convince May at first, and make her ready to leave the beach. In this situation, Shell would need to cope with two challenges: The first challenge was to behave in a way as though there was nothing wrong with May, or that she had been recognized as a sick student by the school consultant. It was obvious that this was complicated and pretending necessitated a subtle tactic. The second challenge was to persuade May that living in the mountains is better than the current location for her.

Shell eventually called May to talk to her one on one, being careful to keep what the consultant had said as a secret. She held May's soft hands in a motherly way, and said, "Sweetie I have exciting news for you! I hope it makes you glad." May asked curiously, "And what is that Mom?" "We want to leave this town and move to a mountain city," Shell replied, "to a new place where you will experience a new school, new teachers, and new friends. You know, my love, we can find a chance to discover a new dimension of our being when we are in a new situation. I can't wait to experience a new life with you there. I am really excited about this decision now. How about you May?" May's eyes were shining brightly, as though she was concentrated on only one thing. Shell was begging her to talk with her eyes and beyond her heavy silence. Finally, Pearl broke the icy silence and said, "Oh Mom, I just hope it has a beautiful warm beach!" Shell had no idea at this moment of what to say; in fact, she was shocked by May's comment. Besides, she discovered that the task was a little more complicated than she had thought. So, she stopped for a moment and tried to relax; and then she added gently and carefully, "Well my girl, I should say that our destination is a mountain; there is no shore, no beach." May responded in a silly, surprised face, "Is there any place other than the sea, the shore, the beach, in the world? Is it possible to find any place without the sea, a shore, or a beach, in the world? Is it possible to live in a place without these? Can we survive without these my Mother?"

Although Shell was feeling very unhappy, her motherhood caused her to put this responsibility on her shoulders and pretend that May is ok. Therefore, she continued smiling, "Oh yes, my pretty! Nature offers so many things in different versions: mountains, seas, deserts, fields, and you should know that each and every place has its own adventures and enjoyment. And all we need to do is to step into the way boldly and bravely while ready to accept new experiences in a new life. I promise you that we will have so many wonderful times together my love!" May just nodded her head, while she remained extremely quiet! This was how May fell apart from the sea; the separation that never became comfortable for May; an isolation which would certainly be painful for May's soul.

Chapter 6
A Mystical Conversation

Caller rushed into the Lord's throne very agitated as it watched the distracting events about to happen to May, and it urged, "Oh Lord! Please do anything for my Pearl, May, or whatever you call her; she is not in a good situation, please save her!" Then the Lord said, "Why do you say 'My Pearl'? Why do you think that she belongs to you?" Caller replied, "I have been considered as the protector of Pearl, haven't I? And I liked this wonderful responsibility the most. You ordered me to stay by her side, to be your voice to her, didn't you?" So the Lord said, "Yes, you are right!" Caller continued, "These beautiful responsibilities which you have had me assume, have made me feel as if Pearl is a major part of me; hence, I love her as much as I love myself. When we become responsible for someone or something, it feels as though some parts of our being melt into another's. Perhaps, the responsibility similar to the flame of love somehow. When we are responsible for someone, it is inevitable to fall in love. Who can deny the correlation between love and responsibility? Pearl and I had so many whispers together during long, lovely conversations. We even experienced a sort of oneness in our travels when we slid along. I became the wings of Pearl, and she became my heart. For these reasons, it seems that it is my obvious right to say 'My Pearl'! You promised to let me stay with Pearl until the end of the story!"

The Lord said, "Well, yes, we did, but we didn't say 'how'. Now tell us directly; what is your concern?" So Caller answered decisively, "I want to be with Pearl; I want to stay by her side. This craving is definitely given to me by you; I was nothing; I had nothing at first; until you poured this fiery temptation into my heart, my gracious God!" Then the Lord asked, "Why are you worried about Pearl? Why are you asking me to save Pearl with so much concern?" So the caller replied, "Because they are thinking that my Pearl, my May is a sick student at her school, while we all know very well that she is not. It seems that she does not have sufficient intelligence to understand her subjects; she is not what she seems. We know how smart she is. This misunderstanding is pushing her away from friends and this is causing her to be alone. I am really worried for her; I want to save her from destroying herself, of stepping down in a way which is not her place, which is far from her divine destiny. I am worried if we push our luck we will lose our chance. I afraid of being late …"

So, Lord said, "You, our dear Caller, I appreciate your concerns! But why do you think that you are kinder than me to Pearl? Here and now I want you to know that your Lord is the kindest and the most compassionate in comparison to anyone else or anything else than you could imagine. I have sometimes heard that some of you say regretfully, 'It would be better if all the creations were created in harmony.' And these people have this regret because they are unable to see the profound reality; they cannot delve deep into the truth. We make issues out of harmony and unity as the lack of harmony and unity is the starting point of all great changes; and changes are the base of evolution; and evolution means move forward to us, to divinity. Therefore, if you scrutinize closely, you will distinguish that what you call distraction is in fact the first step to prosperity. Now, your Pearl your May also is in this procedure. Have you ever seen a mother baking bread? She has to pull and push the dough up and down, and squeeze it well several times just to make it ready for what it must be. Then after so many hits, and ups and downs it must be located in a warm and dark place so that it ferments. What you are worried about is the process that she has to pass through so that she accomplishes the desired form. So stay calm and be patient my precious Caller." But, since the Caller was very persistent, it repeated again, "I want to stay with Pearl. I want to be with her in the real world. I really want to be with her." And the Lord said, "But Pearl is May today; a real human being! She passed successfully all the ups and downs of difficult conflicts of free will and determinism. She is currently living in a body that already died once, and then became alive once more as we commanded. Today, she struggles with so many big problems with her little body; she copes with the problems that are put in her path to qualify her soul in the best way. She confronts the complicated matters which are necessary for her soul's completion, while, as you see, she has a soft and delicate body. But you, my sweet Caller, are not in an objective state yet."

The Caller asked, "Do you remember that I was the wings of the Pearl in the travel of transformation when she was my heart, and I was the dynamic force of flight for her? Was it not an objective state?" Then, Lord answered, "Well you found a heavenly grace at that time; however, it was temporary, and yes you did it, and completed it amazingly! Yet, I believe that you are in a subjective state of existence." "Ok. What can I do to become objective?"

Caller asked. And Lord said, "You are already in an adorable, godly place, where anyone would envy you; you have been the voice by which I could talk to my creatures. You see! Such a high function you have. Moreover, you have been set among the angels, and you have been giving our guidance to our chosen Pearl/May so far. I think that these gifts must be enough for you. What do you think my dear Caller?" At this point, Caller presented its idea in an unwavering voice and said, "I want to be with Pearl, by her side, knee to knee, chest to chest, and shoulder to shoulder. I want to walk on the earth she walks. I want to breathe in the same air that she breathes in. I urge you my God Almighty to give me a pair of eyes so that I become capable to stare at her shiny eyes." Lord said, "Have you forgotten about protection - the first major mission that you are responsible for?" "Your mission is my love, so I put it on my heart. I will take care of her always, everywhere in the best way. Just, Your Majesty, may you tell me how I can achieve this huge grace?"

The Lord said, "The nature of support and protection is Yang. Human beings who I have created have two aspects which are: Yin and Yang. Masculinity is Yang, and femininity is Yin. Therefore, if you want to function as a supporter for her, then you may settle in a male body. Do you agree?" The Caller replied willingly, "I do agree with all of your orders." So, Lord said, "However, as I told you, May's body has already experienced death. For this reason, you may experience death one time as well. Do you agree?" Caller replied, "I do agree with whatever makes me closer to Pearl. Hence, I choose to die just the same as Pearl. Then, I wish to gain the necessary relationship with her." Lord said, "Consequently we will give you a manly body that is perfectly healthy and attractive. Then we will gradually settle you in the same land where May is, and you will breathe the same air that May does. And we will give you a pair of glittering eyes the same as May's. However, you will become May's neighbor while she is still a teenager, while she is far from the sea, offshore, and the beach. As a result, her innate intuition will be hidden just like a forgotten treasure."

"During this period of time, she has lost her spiritual 'self', and she has forgotten her mission. And she is just focusing on her earthly activities. Of course, these physical-earthly activities are the exact necessary passages that must be passed through as it is our obligation, so no need to worry, that she becomes qualified to reach the path of glory; to the highest levels of paradise. Then, when you find her a naughty teenager, you will give her the spiritual warning which is: 'Nether caste ye youre pearls before swine.' And she will ask you as usual, 'What did you say?' And you will answer, 'Don't cast your pearls before swine!' But May, who has hardly been surrounded by daily routines and irrelevant people, will not pay attention to your spiritual warning; although words can always have a wonderful effect. Again you will suggest her cooperation in a job, and you will want her to start a common business, as she is a professional artist even though she is still so young. But she will still behave in a manner as though her eyes are captured with the veil of ignorance, and unable to see you at all. Thus, she will simply refuse your suggestion. Now you will see that all the chances are unsuccessful, so you will become disappointed, still worried about her lost inspirational gifts."

"You will get a broken heart from so much insincerity that she displays towards you. As a result, you will decide to leave the town, and move to a coastal city, which is extremely far away from May's place. Then you will shed so many tears, as you will find out that you, yourself has a frustrated broken heart, as you understand in your loneliness that your Divine mission has not yet been completed. Finally, these blue feelings will draw you toward swimming in the sea on a day when the weather is terrible. And you will never come back home, because you will become drawn here! The great day that you fly towards us, while you have an invaluable gem of love inside your chest. Yes, we respectfully receive true lovers in our realm. Do you agree my Caller?" Caller replied, "I love this romantic destiny that you have composed for me." So the Lord said, "Well, we promise that you will walk in another wonderful masculine body, because you are still in love. Besides, your divine mission is incomplete yet. So it is up to me to give you the grace of life one more time. And I do! You will find another chance to be with May; this time, however, you have passed all the procedures that were necessary to make you communicate with May."

Accordingly, the entire written destiny was performed with all the details; Caller attained a physical body for a while, and lived on the planet for some years. But he died, because there was so much grief and affliction in his heart. However, the Lord Almighty had rewarded this unreturned love with the second gift of life.

Chapter 7

Unification

"I soon realized that no journey carries one far unless,
as it extends into the world around us, it goes an equal
distance into the world within."

Lillian Smith

"Wake up Pearl! Stand up, our chosen gem! Don't be late! You must step out. Your mission is not to be aloof; otherwise you will never come out of your shell. So get up Pearl. Wake up, Pearl."

"Wake up, May. Get up my sweetie! It's time to go to college. You need to get ready." "I'm awake. I had a strange dream, mom." "What was it my sweetie?" asked Shell. "Someone was calling me, and saying something important. The voice was calling me by another name," May said. "Which name?" asked mom. "I don't know. I can't remember the name or the important warning. I need to think; I should try to remember it. But the voice of the caller was buffered by yours; your voices became one in a split second." So Shell said, "However, you will remember it later when your mind becomes relaxed. But now you must get ready so as not to lose your class in the college my dear."

"If a man does not keep pace with his companions, perhaps it is because he hears a different drummer. Let him step to the music which he hears, however measured or far away." Thoreau

There was a lecture in the overcrowded hall of the

Faculty of Art, and most of the students were just walking around, talking, coming and going and they were not paying attention to what the lecturer was saying. In fact, it was difficult to find someone who was listening to him:

"First of all it is preferable to investigate music itself. According to some philosophies, the essence of music, as an intuitive art, is from the cosmos, and it is absorbed by an enlightened spirit of the human being as a flow of energy. Then, after some adjustment, it comes to the earth in audio. That is how it corresponds to the essence of human beings. Therefore, it cannot be isolated from him or her, and it will accompany him or her as an everlasting gift."

"On the other hand, as a humanistic art, music has manifested itself as an identification through different nationalities. In other words, the nature of music has been affected by the regional, linguistic, cultural, and even religious characteristics of countries. Traditional music has a paramount role in identifying different aspects of a nation. As a result, many issues can be understood from it; but how do the people know love? What is their concept of love? For instance, it has a mysterious meaning in Eastern philosophies, while it is simply a term of sensuality in some other philosophies."

"Overall, the only thing which will never change is change itself; during the centuries, music has been always changing, and if we regard it as an abstract language, it is going to shift to a wider global truth. The masterpieces are beyond the border of nationalities these days, and the new generation has found a tendency towards this new version of art. As a matter of fact, the new international music which can be heard everywhere is a symbol of the human desire to integrate - the ultimate goal. So the acceptance of this converted kind of art – international music - will help us align with other people all around the world."

One of May's classmates who was sitting next to her

asked, "What does the lecturer mean by 'universal music?'" "Well, I'm not sure, but maybe he was pointing out that music, which has gone beyond borders, has been accepted by people with different backgrounds and nationalities. For example, like the English language which is a tool through which people can communicate with different cultures and languages, international music could be a means that connect peoples' hearts together regardless of their nationality, language, or culture." Then she stood up after her comment in order to leave the overcrowded place. "Bye!" May said to her classmate, but her classmate asked her, ignoring her goodbye, "Where are you going May?" "I am going to go to the temple that is over the mountains," May replied. So the classmate continued, "Do you want me to come with you? I can if you like!" But May answered, "No thanks, my friend. This noisy place has made me frustrated. For this reason, I prefer to be alone for some time." The classmate was following May's worried eyes. She felt that May was truly agitated. Besides, she was scared because May had chosen to go to the temple alone.

May's mind was overflowing with so many questions throughout the journey along the stony and rocky path toward the temple, "Why is unification the ultimate goal? Is integration or unification really achievable?" Then, while she was climbing up the rocks and stones with some difficulty, she prayed deep inside herself, and requested God to help her to comprehend the answers to her questions. Perhaps, there was a cosmic inner sound that she was listening to and felt in her gut; a higher caller that was warning her that this is a momentous question which has a vital answer which might change so many things.

Sometimes, when we are moving towards a sensational destination, in our super senses, we can strongly smell the fragrances, and hear the sounds of the place right before we get there. May was about to reach the temple when she stopped walking so she could take a deep breath. But, at that moment she found out that her miraculous mind was refreshed from the intoxicating aroma of the temple and the chants of the birds of the temple's garden as she continued along the path now more tempted than ever to reach her goal.

She was hoping to grab a golden opportunity to focus her eyes on the beauty of the temple, to purify her ears with the soft and lovely melody of the birds, and to rejuvenate her soul with the pleasant presence of angels. She was full of hope to receive an answer from heaven to her question, which was as warm as the flames of fire in her impatient heart.

May finally reached the temple. She took off her shoes gently, and she stepped over the cool stony ground lightly. Meanwhile she felt an amazing connection between the soles of her feet and the generous stones. Just like a kind mother who has opened her arms widely to receive her tired child who has just returned home, an affectionate mother who clears the dust of life off her child by her kindness, the abundant mother of earth was drawing the old unpleasant energies out of May's feet and converting them to fresh, revitalizing energy. May was focused on what was going on with her feet when she discovered that the atmosphere of the temple was not what it used to be. There really was a difference now. As a result, she decided to raise her head up to see her surroundings more clearly.

May's instincts were right. There was a stranger at the corner of the temple. The temple space where there used to be a safe ashram, a place to escape to, to get away from the crowd, now it was an ambiguous space that had enthusiastically welcomed a new guest. The presence of a tall, masculine body which was bent forward respectfully with closed eyes caused May to be silent and polite. More than ever. It seemed as if the new guest of the temple felt the presence of someone as well. He realized that someone was nearby, and this caused him to pick up his head, open his eyes, and turn his eyes towards May. Although the temple was full of silence, the pilgrims' hearts were full of unspoken words; May heard a bright dialogue deep inside her heart; so did the new stranger. "Look at this blue sky, how shiny, smooth, and endless it is; how cloud free it is. Keep this image in your heart, just keep in your mind the blue sky which has no clouds."

May's eyes were like a pair of glittering pearls, shaking in a deep blue dream. The two people stared at each other as would people who used to know each other for a long time. Their eyes looked like shimmering bulbs that were burning! Modest May had no idea what to do at this heavy moment. The large reflection of their inner conversation was about to be unfolded when the new man broke the ice and started to talk, "Hello! My name is Marco. My colleagues call me Marco Polo because I travel so much." Then he stopped talking, and looked at May in a way that showed her it was her turn to talk. "Hello! My name is May. I often come to this temple right after the tedious hours of my classes in college, in order to get away from the noise, and recharge my batteries. But I have never seen you here before, inside the temple.' "Well, um yes! This is the first time that I have come here, and there is a long interesting story," Marco said. They got into a very long, spontaneous discussion. "What story?" May inquired. And Marco answered, "I had a near death experience in an accident. Others say that I was in a comma in a hospital. However, I cannot remember anything else. They say that my mother cried very much, prayed hard, and finally invoked God, and requested for a miracle that would make me alive again. Then she saw herself here in this temple while she was dreaming. My mother knew the place because it is near to our house. She said that, 'The temple became as the mountains of glorious lights, and I was gazing at the brightness with astonishment. Meanwhile, I heard a soft voice that promised me my son's survival!' I became conscious a little bit after my mom's dream although I still had so many scars from the accident all over my body. After my recovery, my mother asked me to come to this temple for acknowledgment of the miracle. She believes that my healing has occurred in this holy place." May had a smile on her sweet face, "So we both regard this temple as a shelter and escape, a place to heal our scars!" "Which scars do you mean?" Marco asked. May replied, "Well, you to heal your body scars, and me, to heal scars on my heart!"

"Many people believe in scars on the heart," Marco said in a gentle voice, "but I don't. I believe that they are warning signs about precious experiences in the past, and at the present time warning us to be a powerful and smart, not vulnerable and stupid; they are memorials of life's complicated moments which strengthen our soul for the future." May dropped her eyes down, and did not say anything. Marco didn't know if she agreed with him. A heavy silence confronted them once again. This caused May to start talking, but this time with a different subject, just to change the tempo.

"My mind was actually busy on a problem before I got to the temple." "And what was that?" Marco asked eagerly. May said that "There was a lecture in the college hall and the subject was music. I think the lecturer believed that unification is the ultimate goal. Now, what has made me confused is why unification is the ultimate goal. Or, is unification achievable at all?" Marco deliberated for a while, and then he said, "Well, let's not concern ourselves about the lecture. But what sort of unification do 'you' mean?

Or let me ask my question in a more direct way: What do you mean by unification, May?" May responded, "To reach oneness!" Marco asked, "Oneness of lovers?" May replied, "I don't wonder about oneness of someone with someone, or someone with something. But my question is unification itself. I want to know about the essence of it." So Marco explained, "In my point of view unification is unity, when two souls reach to the same point, travel beyond the limitation of barriers of time and space, and melt in together beyond any natural rules, so far that their souls become indistinguishable, and they turn into one." May listened to him carefully. Then she said, "I think it's time to go." Marco said, "May I come to you and accompany you to your home?" May said, "No thank you. My house is far from the temple."

The blue eyes of Marco became deeper and he said, "The longer the better," May smiled while she blushed with shame. Then she continued, "However I know some shortcuts, so we can make the way shorter,". Marco said, "I don't want any shortcuts at this moment. I seek the longest way when I'm walking with such a sweet lady. We would both enjoy the journey itself; the inspiration that surrounds us. You know May, destination is awesome after such an inspirational path." Then they started walking towards May's house; they were talking nonstop throughout the journey. When they got to the destination, May stopped in a way as if she was about to say goodbye. Because Marco's heart was connected to May's, somehow he felt something, so he started talking before leaving her, "I want to see you again!" May kept quiet at first. But after a moment she said, "I will come to the temple again, so we will." Each of them went their separate ways, while their hearts were on fire each and every moment. They both believed, in their loneliness, that whatever they said and heard already existed somehow in their old memories; nothing that happened was new; there was nothing new. Remembering the moments that they experienced together was like an antique treasure which was just discovered in their souls. The glamour of May's eyes reminded Marco of a pure, tempting pearl. And the deep blue of Marco's eyes reminded May of a bright blue sky without a single cloud!

Desire is always the starting point of a lovely conversation, wanting is always the cause of attracting lovers to a rendezvous, and the flames of hearts consistently act like magnets. The next day, May decided to go to the temple after the end of her classes. But her motivation was not to escape into a cave of loneliness this time. On the contrary, she was drawn toward there by the blaze of her burning heart, impatiently; as though it was not her, but a heavenly cart pulling her to a magnificent celebration which was held in the highest points in the sky.

May finally reached the temple, although the way seemed much longer than ever. When she entered into the temple, she found Marco there impatiently waiting for her. Marco said, "Hello." May replied, "Hello." "How are you doing? How are you feeling today?" Marco asked May. May replied, "I'm doing well, thanks. I have a strange feeling; I used to be aloof, getting away from people, running out of crowds. Now something odd was attracting me here like a magnet." "How about your heart?" Marco asked, "Do you like this feeling deep inside your heart?" May said, "Well, I used to be on my own. Loneliness had become a habit for me as I used to have sweet conversations there. I used to prefer loneliness, not because I was interested in staying alone, but because these lovely inner talks were definitely inspiring and upliftings. I actually love people. And I don't care who they are. I love them for no reason. Yet, I have been falling apart as my talks, my words, and my behavior become unusual. Communication was difficult for me. But it seems that this problem is gone now; I can say that it's become very different now. I am confused, because this is the first time that I am eager for conversation." Marco smiled and said, "But I didn't think of communication, conversation, talk, and so on and so forth, when I wanted to come here. The only concern that I had was just seeing you again. Besides, I have been thinking about your mental conflict; your important question since last time." "Unification you mean?" May questioned curiously. And Marco answered, "Yes." So May continued, "I didn't understand why the lecturer put forward music and unification in relationship to each other. I mean, I don't know how they are related to each other; or are they really interconnected or two separate issues?" So Marco explained, "Well, I think there are some tools and means for human beings through which they can connect to the higher aspects of the universe. Art is one of the most powerful tools for getting higher in the sky, I believe. I also believe that no masterpieces would have been created unless the artist becomes one with the source of creation. In other words, each and every manifestation of art is the display of the marvelous moment of unity with Lord Almighty. By the way, why do you think that discussing music as an art, and unification is something extraordinary May? I strongly believe that the mission of art is to unify our essence."

"May I would never think that our meeting is a new moment in my life. I feel this is an old event that has been always with me. And I feel there was a hidden piece in my soul that has been discovered. I don't think that your 'self' is out of my 'self'; I think that you are a major part of my soul. I have been focusing on your question since you have mentioned it, and I have been thinking about that all the time." "But it was my question, why should it make you so concerned? Why should it make your mind as busy as mine?" May asked. Marco explained, "Have you ever looked at rings of string? We are all creatures like these connected rings of string if we look closely. If one of us falls down, others will as well. Conversely, if one of us flies high, he or she will certainly pull high the other colleagues with him or her as well. So don't think that what has made your mind confused is not related to mine. And, have no doubt that if you find the answer to your question, and if this mental spark grows stronger, I will also get to the same level as you. Your ascension is my ascension. We are all riding the same ship towards the same goal. So, it is natural to experience the same happiness and sadness, ups and downs, and highs and lows throughout the path."

May was paying full attention to what Marco was saying. Marco continued, "I hope I have successfully cleared the matter of unification in your mind." Then he became silent. May said, "Yes, you did it well! I feel words and terms have never been as clear and bright as this. I have never experienced such a conversation. I felt something that I have never felt in any other discussion!" "And what was that?" Marco asked eagerly. May replied, "Joy and happiness. I feel you said just what I have been always seeking; what I have desired so much. The truths that you revealed to me were the exact answers to my prayers, Marco. You answered whatever I had questioned in my loneliness." Marco stopped her and said, "Do you know that I breathe differently when I'm with you May? I inhale and exhale in a way that I have never done before. My heartbeats play a love song when I am with you. I am intoxicated by your presence, May, and I cannot understand how time seems to fly." May's face got as pink as a mildewed rose, as she was a shy girl, and Marco's words were playing with her heart. So she turned her beautiful pearly eyes down to the ground, and kept quiet. Again, a heavy silence filled the air, and it was the sad indication of the time to leave. Yes, they patiently left the place, aware that their flaming heart would pull them to the temple once more.

May and Marco spent many sweet times together, and they both knew that nothing and nowhere could be like this. By now, they knew that there could be no more excitement except when they were together and since then happiness meant togetherness.

It was as if that the whole world was gathered right in the temple and there was no more motivation in life other than standing up, getting ready, and moving toward the temple. May walked to the temple almost without explanation as to why she was going there. May's heart was beating in a different way; as if it was beating an epic rhythm, like a spring chant, soft and fascinating. Rough and tough rocks and stones of the path were all converted to soft and comfortable clouds of the sky. These glorious meetings helped May hear the songs of the birds better than ever. May entered the temple enthusiastically to see Marco but this time Marco was not there. There was no one else there. The temple was empty and full of silence and loneliness. Silence and loneliness was May's favorite once when she used to go to the temple hurriedly seeking it out; now it brought a heavy grief as heavy as the stones. She didn't know what she would do faced with this unexpected situation. Inevitably, she waited for Marco until sunset, but nothing happened. No one came. May started mourning to God as she became very discouraged, "Oh dear God, this way of life, this being aloof, this staying alone in silence had become my lifestyle, and I was content with it; I had no complaints! Then Marco came to my life, and this happy event changed everything. After that, I was not seeking loneliness at all. Unexpectedly, his sweet presence fulfilled my life's dream, and his absence would become as bitter as bile, as we experienced joyful moments that nothing would ever equal. I am confident that he is definitely eager for me; I saw it in the depth of his blue eyes. So God, please tell me why he is not here for our rendezvous now? Where is he? Is he fine? Is he sick? Is he hurt? Did I do anything wrong that made him stop coming here to see me again?" Only God knew what May was feeling, and how difficult the time passed for her impatient heart.

The next day, May opened her eyes, and seeing Marco was the first strong desire that she had. Without any hesitation, she decided to go to the temple. But again Marco was not there; May didn't find Marco as she hoped. She went back home agitated and depressed. Then her knees weakened and she moaned, "Oh Lord! time without Marco is as a horrible static monster, and it is going to take my breath from my body. It would be the end of time for me if I don't see Marco once more. In my lexicon, apocalypse meant when I can no longer see him. I had barely stepped out of my cave of loneliness in order to live my life for Marco. He was as epic as Shakespeare's poetry to me. Oh God, this overcoming of loneliness has purified every single part of my soul, the flash of his love has cleared any fear from my mind, and the hope of seeing him again has made me unwavering! I bet he is not aware of these treasures that have generously been given to me. Now Lord, I request you to calm down my fiery heart as I can't tolerate it any more."

As May was moaning and crying, she suddenly fell asleep. Then she saw herself in a dream with Marco in a heavenly endless garden. The garden was full of beautiful, amazing herbs, and the two were walking around, and enjoying themselves. Suddenly, something captured May's attention; she found an unusual herb, and she cheerfully showed it to Marco, "I found the secret of longevity which the ancient people were always trying to discover." Marco stared at May and said, "Yes! We found the elixir of longevity. As a matter of fact, love is the elixir of longevity itself; I intuitively know that love breaks the physical and normal processes, and leads towards the uppermost path. It means that lovers go beyond the limitations of time and space." Suddenly she opened her eyes and found her worried mother standing at her bedside.

May kept going to the temple every day, hoping to see Marco. Without Marco, the temple was now the ultimate of unhappiness and solitude for May. This separation lasted forty days and forty nights. Finally, Marco came back to her after forty-one days and they hugged and kissed each other, and they shed tears as they were extremely overjoyed to see each other one more time.

May talked to Marco in a loving way, "Where have you been? What have you been doing? I missed you! I was really worried about you. I was confident deep inside my heart that we would see each other again, and that this grief would turn to joy and happiness. I don't like to be alone anymore. I don't know how I can stand being without you." Marco responded to her in an affectionate way as well, "I missed you very much too, May! You were the first desire of my burning heart when I was waking up in the early morning. I remembered each and every moment. Passing time was as hard as torture. Meanwhile, I could imagine clearly that you were feeling sad. But May, believe me that I was unable to come here to see you in the temple because it was a Divine order for me to stay in solitude in an isolated place for forty days. I did it for the Lord's sake, although my heart was like a fiery bush burning for you."

"Now it is time to tell you the happy news. As you will discover, all of our efforts will be definitely rewarded; I have received a heavenly message in the last day of my solitude which recalls you and me to their realm and to a mystical ceremony that will be held specifically for you and me." May had no idea what Marco was talking about. So she asked, "What are you talking about? Whose realm do you mean? Where is their realm? Why do they hold a ceremony?" Marco answered, "Both of us are supposed to get ready, and travel towards a coastal city, and wait at the land and sea border. I know as much as you do about the content of the ceremony and what will go on there. But I want to assure you that there must be a precious gift for you and me after this forty-day purification of our beings." But again we will have to face the barriers of our mothers: the mourning of mothers who have been our warm homes!

"I express my grief to you vividly, and frankly. How can I hide it? I used to take care of you all night long, and prepare for your needs all day long. I harmonized my being with yours with all my love, and I cuddled you gently so that I protected you against any danger. How could you leave me while you have grown this much in my tender hands? How could you travel? What didn't I do for you? What emotion did I deprive you from? Why are you so full of this temptation? Temptation of motion! Have you any concern about me after your leaving?"

Although it was not easy, they convinced their mothers with much love and kindness: "Oh mother! You are the most beautiful angel on the planet in my eyes. You are so unique in pureness and softness. I always adore you, and I am proud of you! Stay calm for the sake of goodness, because I can't see the flames in your heart. I know that this path, this separation is not easy. But be sure my mom that you will be elevated too, as there is a confident and supportive observer who wonders about all of us. So mom! Please try to be tolerant as we need to go because this path must be followed!"

Willingly, they obeyed the Divine Order after the complicated pleading with the descendent angels, their mothers. They left behind their possessions, their lands, and everything else, towards the sea.

It was 11:11 am on Friday when they reached the land

and sea border. At this point, they were ordered to stop moving forward and to wait. So they did and took off their shoes respectfully, and knelt on the ground. Then, the desire for listening embraced them from tip to toe when a heavenly sound addressed them:

"Welcome to my throne my great lovers. We are so proud of you here. I summon you both to my realm to announce to you our Cosmos plan which is organized for you in our System of Creation. But I have to describe some things first."

"The first issue is 'True Love.' I assessed and examined your love several times; in other words, I challenged you through ups and downs, confidence and doubts, free will and determinism, trial and error, and so many other situations. Never think that this was for our own benefit. Never! As we already have the Ultimate Knowledge about your whole beings, because I am your Great Creator; whoever creates a masterpiece, then he would control and be the whole of it, and understand what is what. I want to say that you, as my masterpieces, are crystal clear to me. I, in fact, confronted you with these ups and downs, confidence and doubts, free will and determinism, and trial and error, to inform you about your skills and abilities. Because when you know yourselves better, you certainly know me, and this knowledge is a graceful bliss. For example, I set you apart for some time, and then I monitored you to see if you were able to tolerate this isolation, though you lived your life with commitment, it was definitely clear that there was something missing, as if you hardly breathed without each other; you felt like there was no painkiller for your heartache; sleeplessness didn't leave you all night long. However, when we brought you together, you found out that rejoicing and happiness surrounded you, and you were embraced with prosperity and abundance. We call this sort of affection 'Pure Love' or 'True Love'; supremely spiritual emotions which are beyond any fear, jealousy, or demands, and full of braveness, affection, compassion, and grace. When you love each other, without selfish reasons, all the foggy veils will be cleared, understanding will become higher, and consciousness will explode; Marco becomes May and May becomes Marco; two indistinguishable humans! We call this 'Unconditional Love' in our kingdom, which is absolutely hard to achieve. If I want to delve into a deeper layer, I would say that this unconditional love has been already located in the essence of every existence, but, unfortunately it is mostly a neglected gift which would rarely be exploited from their essences. But, now I am proud to announce to you that you both, May and Marco, have discovered, utilized, and appreciated it the most. Yes, you did! So congratulations as you have been prosperous so far."

"The second issue is that you, my dear lovers, have been always following not only our abstract but also our concrete guidance. In the day and in the night, in the silence and in the crowd, in sadness or happiness you have been listening to us politely, accepting our inspirations contentedly, and believing that this is the best path to step onto. Although our guidance is sometimes a bizarre voice to humans that seems as if it leads them to nowhere, you have been the brave hearts with unwavering belief. When the innate guidance is received patiently, naturally, and regularly, then the 'Evolution' happens. Of course the hierarchy of the evolution is absolutely a personal matter. Yet, so many traditional or religious systems insist on classifying it, and preparing a standardized pattern to different people with different natures. This causes human beings to lose their innate treasures which have originally been given to them as a gift called 'intuition'. They would never follow their inner guidance, and gradually the sense of discrimination from right and wrong dies in their beings. Sad! And proudly I called you here to say that you both never let these worldly systems interfere or destroy your awareness. This courage and bravery made your souls like a purified canal through which any universal message could be transferred."

"The third issue is 'Unification in Love' or 'Love Unification'. It is about the people who live their lives in a loving, altruistic way; the people who simply behave according to their soul; they adore whatever they have and whoever they know, while they don't have any logical reason if you ask them why. In other words, they love anything and anyone just for no reason.

Interestingly, 'Love' is the base of unification. And now you might ask me how. Well, when people are in love, they break the boundaries of their 'selves' and this means that 'ego' is withdrawn completely. When ego withdraws, gut feelings stimulate, intuition rejuvenates, inner reality thrives, and consciousness expands as much as our throne. This is where the soul unifies with God. This accomplishment is called 'the oneness of man and God', and this process is called 'Love Unification'. Unified people are the ones who receive angelic guidance from the heavens easily while they regard it as the wisest and the most confident way. They realize rationally that the godly path is the most beautiful direction that they could choose. From the perspective from where they stand, following this wisdom is nothing but love itself."

"Now it is time to announce to you our Cosmos Plan, to you, my amazing lovers who embraced each other with true unconditional love and became clairvoyant under the shower of our guidance. Love, in fact, is the light of my presence. Whenever two people love each other, it is like burning lanterns in a fascinating marble house! Yes, you are such a beautiful brilliant and blazing perspective for us. It is obvious that such a glowing appearance could be a pathfinder that illuminates the way for other wayfarers, and leads them towards the destination. In other words, I raise you up as "Light" workers, and send you to my people to enlighten them with your 'love light,' connect them to the Source of Light; also to act like mediums, a bridge between heavenly and earthly creatures. In addition, I want you to receive the mourning of broken hearts, and deliver their whispers and prayers to the sky, and then receive the responses from heaven, and give them back to them as a healing. Furthermore, receive my warnings to awake neglected people on the planet so that you bring them back to a happy life. I want you to become a beautiful canal between suffering persons and healer angels. So step out of your limitations boldly, and find your way through your Divine life's mission; staying aloof has never been your destiny. Be sure that you will never be on your own, because we will protect you as a pair of shells which cuddle the pearl lovingly and constantly, and will accompany you in hurricanes, and horrible ocean waves, as if you are a compassionate boat alone on the surface of the lonely sea."

"Good Luck My Enlightened Workers on the Planet!" Light up the world!

Such Adorable Creations You Are!

www.ingramcontent.com/pod-product-compliance
Lightning Source LLC
Chambersburg PA
CBHW022108040426
42451CB00007B/183